D1607226

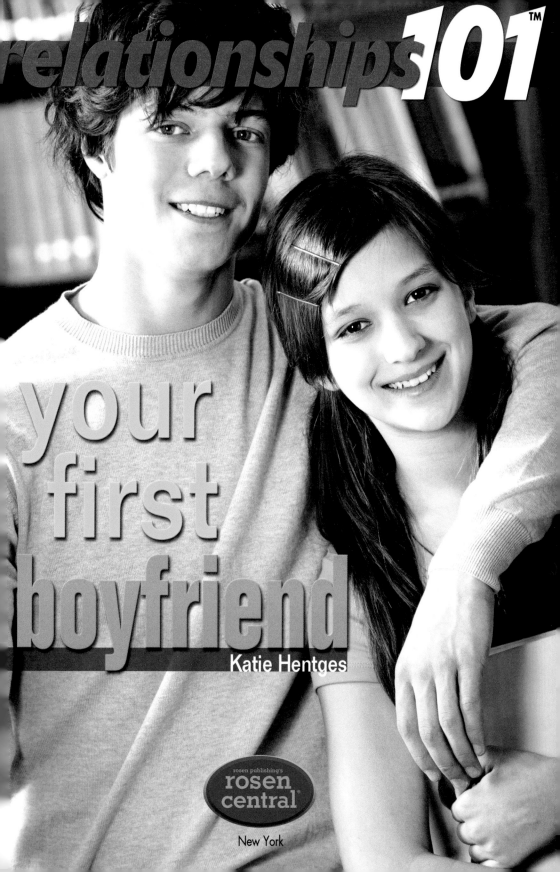

relationships 101™

your first boyfriend

Katie Hentges

rosen publishing's
rosen central®

New York

Published in 2013 by The Rosen Publishing Group, Inc.
29 East 21st Street, New York, NY 10010

First Edition

Library of Congress Cataloging-in-Publication Data

Hentges, Katie.
Your first boyfriend/Katie Hentges.—1st ed.
    p. cm.—(Relationships 101)
Includes bibliographical references and index.
ISBN 978-1-4488-6829-2 (library binding)—
ISBN 978-1-4488-6833-9 (pbk.)—
ISBN 978-1-4488-6837-7 (6-pack)
1. Interpersonal relations in adolescence—Juvenile literature. 2. Man-woman relationships—Juvenile literature. 3. Dating (Social customs)—Juvenile literature. 4. Teenage girls—Juvenile literature. I. Title.
BF724.3.I58H44 2013
158.20835—dc23

2012003284

Manufactured in the United States of America

CPSIA Compliance Information: Batch #S12YA: For further information, contact Rosen Publishing, New York, New York, at 1-800-237-9932.

CONTENTS

introduction

It may not have been that long ago that the idea of having a boyfriend seemed silly. You and your friends might have had crushes, but the boys you liked didn't seem to care much about girls. But now you see kids in your grade dating. Boys seem to notice you more. Maybe you've met a boy you really like and you'd like to start dating, too.

It seems simple. You meet a boy, you like him, you ask him out, he says "yes," and then you live happily ever after. But most of the time, it's not that simple. How do you know he likes you? How do you ask him out? Where do you go on dates? What happens if you fight? What if you have to break up? Even adults have these questions, but it's often harder for young people to get answers to them. Their friends haven't had much experience, either, and can't always give advice. There are tons of Web sites, magazine articles, and books about relationships, but most of them are for adults. Older people often don't take younger people's relationships seriously, and besides, it can be embarrassing to ask adults relationship questions.

Hopefully this book can answer some of your questions. Of course, no two people are exactly alike, and no two relationships are going to be the same, but it's always good to have some basic guidelines.

This book discusses:

- How to get to know a boy
- How to ask him out
- How to deal with rejection
- How to make a relationship stronger
- How to deal with conflict
- How to deal with breakups

Of course, this book doesn't have all of the answers. Nobody will. The most important thing to remember is that having a boyfriend should be about having fun and enjoying the time you spend together.

CHAPTER ONE

YOU LIKE HIM!

Maybe you've been friends for a while. Maybe you've had a couple of classes with him. Maybe you've just seen him in the halls and thought he was cute. Whatever the case may be, you know that you like him and you want to get to know him better. But how do you do that?

Get Closer

If you've talked to him only a few times or have just seen him around, it's a good idea to try to get to know him a little better. Then, you can decide if you two would make a good couple. Plus, it increases your chances that he'll say yes if you ask him out.

Here are some ways to get to know him better:

• Ask your friends if they know him or any of his friends. If so, they might know more about him and could introduce you to him.

Get to know your crush better by working with him on a school project. You'll both have a great chance to show off your creativity and intelligence.

- If you have a class together, make an effort to try and talk to him before or after class. (It may be hard to do, but make sure you pay attention to your schoolwork during class.)
- Walk up and introduce yourself. This may be scary, but it shows that you can be outgoing and friendly. It also shows that you're interested in him, although he may not pick up on that right away.

It's not a good idea to:

- Get his number from someone else and call/text him out of the blue. Most people don't like to get random calls from strangers or near-strangers. It's better to get his number from him directly or find another way to contact him.
- Show up somewhere he likes to hang out with his friends (like a skate park) if you've

Don't text your crush unless you've gotten to know him first and he tells you it's OK. Texting him without permission could cause a lot of confusion and embarrassment.

never been there before. You'll probably wind up pretending to be someone you're not, which is never the start of a good relationship. Or worse, he might think you're stalking him!

Keep in mind that it might be hard to get closer to him at first, especially if you see him only when he's around friends. Boys can be shy and insecure. Just a few years ago, a lot of them probably thought you had cooties. It may take some time before you feel like the time is right to ask him out.

If you've tried to talk to him a few times and it's like talking to a brick wall, it's probably time for you to move on. Don't take it personally—he may just not be interested in talking to girls yet. It's better to spend your time with friends having fun than trying to go after a guy who isn't really interested.

WHAT IF I LIKE AN OLDER GUY?

It's not hard to see why you might get a crush on an older guy. They seem more mature and ready for a relationship than guys in your age group. But you can run into a lot of problems dating an older boy. He probably has more relationship experience than you. He may expect more from you, emotionally and sexually, than you're ready for, no matter how mature you are. Also, an older guy may be attracted to younger girls because he thinks they're easy to control. Even if you're not easy to control, you don't want to be with someone who thinks you are. So, while it's fine to admire older guys from far away, it's better to stick with boys your own age. There will be plenty of time for serious, mature relationships in the future.

Does He Like You That Way?

Let's say you've been able to spend a little time with your crush and you two are getting along well. You want him to be your boyfriend, but you're not sure if he wants the same thing. How do you know?

- He does things to try and impress you, like playing an instrument or showing how athletic he is.
- He talks to you more than other girls.
- He jokes with you more than other girls.
- He compliments you.
- He asks you questions about your interests, your family, etc.
- He touches you, stands close to you, or makes other physical contact with you

Guys often show off their musical skills to girls they like. Did your crush play guitar for you? That's a good sign that he wants to be your boyfriend.

(as long he doesn't get into your personal space in a way that makes you feel uncomfortable).

- He tells your friends he likes you, or his friends tell you that he likes you.
- He says he likes you when you ask.

Asking Him Out

People used to believe that girls should never ask guys out. Luckily, you live in a time when it's common to do so. If you're ready to start going out with a guy, don't wait for him to ask. Some boys are shy. Other boys

MY FRIEND AND I LIKE THE SAME GUY

Friends share a lot, but they don't usually share boyfriends. If you and your friend have a crush on the same guy and you want to ask him out, you should talk to her first. If she's supportive, then great! If she tells you that she doesn't want you to ask him out or she seems upset, the best thing is to avoid asking him out.

If you do ask him out, you face the possibility of ruining your friendship. It would be great if you could have your boyfriend and your friend, too, but it's unfair to expect her to put her feelings aside. It's up to you to decide how important your friendship is. If you do decide to ask him out, be honest with her about it. It would be more upsetting for her to hear about it from someone else.

Always keep in mind that most friendships will last longer than your relationship. Most of the time it's not worth it to sacrifice a friend in order to date a guy.

are clueless about girls. It's better for you to take a chance instead of waiting around for him. It may be a little scary, but at least you will know for sure if he likes you or not.

So you've worked up the courage to ask him out. How should you do it?

You can go through friends, text him, or write him a note, but a good way to ask him out is to call him on the phone. An even better way is to ask him face-to-face. Getting someone else to ask for you or talking to him electronically is easier, but face-to-face communication shows you're confident in yourself and interested in him.

It's also a good idea to try to ask him out as privately as possible. This way, both of you won't feel pressure from other people. He can accept or reject your request without either of you feeling embarrassed. It can be difficult, but even if you can pull him away for a moment in the hall at school, that's better than asking in front of all of his or your friends.

The actual words you use to ask him out should be your own. Basically, you should just be honest and straightforward and tell him that you like him and that you'd like to go out sometime. If you're really nervous, you might want to rehearse asking him out a few times before you actually do it. You can practice alone, but sometimes rehearsing in front of a friend is good, too. She (or he) can give you pointers about what to say.

Going Out

He said yes! Now what do you do?

Dating in middle school is usually pretty casual. Your parents (or his parents) may not want you to go on any one-on-one dates yet. Even if they do let you go on dates alone, you may not have

School dances can be a great way to get to know your boyfriend. They're fun and romantic, but they're also chaperoned so your parents will worry less.

enough money to do much more than go for a walk or get some fast food.

If you can't go on dates, hanging out in a group of friends is a good way to get to know him better. There are always school dances, lock-ins, and other chaperoned events. Going to the park or over to someone's house to watch a movie is a good way to spend time with him, too. Whatever you do, make sure you're both having a good time.

What If He Says No?

Nobody likes being rejected. It can be discouraging and humiliating. It may hurt your self-esteem. But everyone has been rejected at some point in time, no matter how beautiful or charming they may be. Being rejected doesn't mean that there's something wrong with you. In fact, he might have his own reasons for saying no that have nothing to do with you. Always remember that your opinion about yourself is more important than anyone else's.

It can hurt, especially if he's rude or cruel to you when he says no. But if he's mean when he turns you down, he probably wouldn't have made a very good boyfriend anyway. Consider yourself lucky. There will be plenty of guys who will appreciate you for who you are.

Sometimes a guy will tell you that he just wants to be friends. The "friend zone" is never a fun place to be, but it happens to a lot of people. Sometimes friendships do turn into relationships, but if he's already said no, it's better to move on. It's OK to have a crush on a friend, but if

you're really hurt or constantly obsessing about him, it's probably a good idea to take a break from your friendship with him. Friendships shouldn't cause you stress. Besides, if you're always thinking about him, you may miss out on a relationship with someone who likes you. Spend time with your other friends instead.

No matter how he acts, if you ask him once and he says no, don't ask again. This can be hard if you really like him, especially if it seems like he's still flirting with you. If things change and he decides he wants to date you after all, he can always ask. You're better off spending your time and energy doing something else.

YOUR RELATIONSHIP

Congratulations! You asked and he said yes, or vice versa. You're in a relationship. Now what do you do?

Have Fun

Asking a boy out can be nerve wracking. Talking about feelings is hard sometimes. Even the word "relationship" can be scary. But even the most "serious" and "mature" relationships that are happy involve fun. You can hang out with friends, go to dances, joke around after school—just have fun together.

Be Yourself

One of the most important things in any relationship is to be yourself. This can be hard when you like someone and you really want him to like you too. You might be tempted to pretend you don't like some of the things you like. You might try to do things to impress him that you

It's normal to feel jealous sometimes, but try not to assume the worst when your boyfriend talks to other girls. Talk to a trusted adult if you feel insecure in your relationship.

wouldn't normally do. Just remember that you want him to like you for who you are, not who you pretend to be.

A boyfriend who is a good fit for you will want you to be yourself as well. You'll feel appreciated and liked more because he knows the real you. You'll feel better about yourself for being honest. You'll both have more fun because you're comfortable. And you'll both feel better about your relation-ship because you'll be able to get closer emotionally.

Be Confident in Your Relationship

You see your boyfriend talking to another girl in English class, and it makes you feel jealous. He doesn't call you when he says he will, and it makes you feel upset. It can be very easy to slip into these patterns when you're in a relationship.

The best rule is just to be confident. You're his girlfriend! That means that he likes you. Don't spend a lot of time worry-ing about how your boyfriend

Talk to a parent, older sibling, or other trusted family member. An older person can often give you a new perspective because he or she may have experienced something similar in the past.

feels about you. If your bad feelings persist, talk to a parent or other trusted adult about how you're feeling. Chances are, he or she felt the same way at some point. It's natural.

Don't Neglect the Rest of Your Life

It's easy to spend all of your time with your boyfriend and lose interest in your friends or other activities you enjoyed before you started dating. But it's good for couples to spend time apart. Your friends were there for you before your relationship and will be there for you after it ends. It's important to keep those friendships strong.

Don't give up the activities you enjoyed before you started dating your boyfriend just to spend more time with him either. If you were into sports or dance or theater before you started dating, keep it up. Your hobbies make you a more well-rounded person. This means that you'll be happier and more mature, which is good for you and can make your relationship even stronger.

You'll probably hear this from your parents and teachers, too, but make sure that you don't neglect your schoolwork either. Boys will come and go, but your education stays with you.

HOW DO I JUGGLE LIFE AND A RELATIONSHIP?

Everybody's busy, not just adults. You may have after-school activities like sports and music lessons. You may have to take care of younger siblings or work on a paper route or at the family business. You probably have chores. And, of course, homework. How do you manage all of this and enjoy time with your boyfriend? Especially when your boyfriend is as busy as you are?

- *Talk when you can. Even just saying "hi" in the hallway to each other between classes can brighten both of your days. If you can, walk each other home from school or ride the bus together.*
- *Find ways to do activities together. If you both play musical instruments, practice together. If you're in a religious youth group, invite him to join. Even just going to events like each other's games and concerts shows that you care and can keep you connected.*
- *Don't stress. Your relationship should be fun. It shouldn't feel like one more thing to squeeze into a busy day. If it's causing more stress than it should, maybe it's time to break up. You can always get back together later when life is less crazy.*

Communicate

Communication can help bring you closer to your boyfriend and resolve conflicts. When you talk on the phone or face-to-face with your boyfriend, you're communicating. If you're writing him notes, texting, or e-mailing him, you're communicating. The best communication usually happens face-to face, especially about important things. But no matter how you're communicating, remember that it's always important to your relationship. And remember that guys are sometimes brought up to communicate differently from girls. This can make it harder for them to express their feelings openly.

Communication isn't just about saying, "Hey, I like you!" It's also about talking about your feelings. Tell him how you're feeling about your relationship, how your relationship with your family is going, how you're feeling in general. All of these things are important for a relationship.

Communicating about your feelings can also help to prevent conflict. It can help your boyfriend find out more about you and the best way to

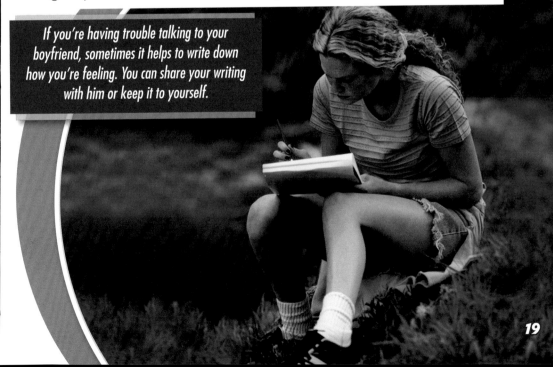

If you're having trouble talking to your boyfriend, sometimes it helps to write down how you're feeling. You can share your writing with him or keep it to yourself.

support you when times are tough. You will also learn a lot about your boyfriend when you communicate. How supportive is he? How does he respond to problems? What things in life are important to him? Knowing these things is important and can help make your relationship stronger.

What About the Physical Relationship?

Sex can be good, but only when you're ready for it. It's up to you to decide what to do based on your beliefs and what makes you comfortable. Just remember a few things when you're considering how far you should go physically with your boyfriend.

Sexual activity (including oral sex) comes with a lot of risks. Those risks are both emotional and physical. It's not fair, but often the risks are higher for girls. Girls are the ones who risk pregnancy and face greater possibility of contracting sexually transmitted infections than boys do.

You may feel a lot of pressure to do things before you're ready. No matter where the pressure comes from, remember that you are the one who experiences the emotional and physical risks, not anyone else. If the pressure comes from your friends, keep in mind that they may be feeling the same pressure themselves. They may even be exaggerating about what they've done in order to seem more mature. But the truly grown-up, mature thing to do is to take time to figure out what feels right for you and to be true to yourself.

If the pressure is coming from your boyfriend, tell him that you're only going to do what you're comfortable with. If he tries to get you to do more by pouting, acting angry, guilt-tripping, or pushing any other buttons, dump him. You'll

Sharing private information online is a major breach of trust. If your boyfriend is sharing private information about you online without your permission, it's time to break up.

"SEXTING"

Some girls take private pictures of themselves and text them to their boyfriends. (This is called "sexting.") They trust their boyfriends to keep the pictures private, but in some cases the boys forward the pictures to their classmates. Guys who share their girlfriends' photos violate their trust and engage in unacceptable and hurtful behavior. Unfortunately, guys often get in less trouble than the girls do. It's best to protect yourself and not send any photos to your boyfriend that you wouldn't want your parents to find out about. No matter how much you trust and like a boy, remember that anything you send electronically can be shared.

Holding hands is a great way for you and your boyfriend to show affection for each other. It also strengthens your bond as a couple, especially if it's during a talk or a walk together.

find another boy who respects you and cares about your feelings.

You may not be feeling pressure from anyone else but still feel like you need to show your boyfriend that he's special to you. You can do this without sex. Hugging, kissing, holding hands, talking, and writing nice notes are all a way of showing your affection and getting close to your boyfriend. Plenty of teens and adults show affection to each other in romantic relationships this way without having sex. Besides, it's a stereotype that all boys want sex. It may be that your boyfriend isn't ready for sex either and will actually be relieved to find out you don't want it yet.

Alternately, any guy who won't take no for an answer is not someone you want to be in a relationship with. If your boyfriend, or any guy, goes any further physically than what you are comfortable with and refuses to stop when you ask him to, he is not respecting your boundaries. Studies suggest that a large majority of sexual assaults among young people occur with someone you know, including boyfriends. Don't be afraid to speak up and say no.

PROBLEMS IN YOUR RELATIONSHIP

Every relationship has its problems. No matter how much you and your boyfriend may like each other, no two people are exactly the same and you're bound to have disagreements. However, if you work on solving your problems together, you might just make your relationship stronger.

There are four steps to solving any problems in your relationship:

1. Identify the problem.
2. Talk about the problem.
3. Come to an agreement on how to solve the problem.
4. Carry out that agreement.

Identifying the Problem

Sometimes identifying the problem is simple. Maybe you want to go out to a movie, but he'd rather go for ice cream. Maybe you forgot his birthday, or maybe he said something that hurt your feelings. These problems may not be simple to solve, but they're easy to understand.

Sometimes problems can be harder to figure out. You and your boyfriend may need some time talking over how you feel before you can understand what the conflict is between you. He may see a problem in the relationship that you didn't think was a problem at all. You may be upset about something he didn't even realize he did. It's important to make sure that both of you know the problem you're talking about before you start trying to discuss it in depth.

Talking About the Problem

The best way to resolve any conflict is to discuss it with your boyfriend face-to-face. Sometimes it's difficult to confront someone, especially if you really like that person, but it's important. Not talking about problems with your boyfriend will affect your happiness and the health of your relationship.

It may seem easier to talk about problems through texts or e-mails or other ways of communicating, but talking in person is best. It shows that

The best way to solve a problem between you and your boyfriend is to sit down and have a talk. You can express yourselves honestly and get the problem out in the open.

you're serious about the problem and helps to avoid misunderstandings.

It's very important that you're honest and upfront about any feelings you have about the situation. But also remember to be objective. If you are angry when you are discussing something with your boyfriend, he will likely get defensive. If you're not sure how you feel about something, tell him that. There's nothing wrong with asking him for a little more time to figure things out. Just make sure that you keep him updated about how you're feeling and what you're thinking. Of course, this doesn't mean that you need to share your every thought with him, but it does mean that you need to be open with him. Similarly, if you want to talk but he says he's not ready, then it's good to give him some time to think. If he doesn't bring up the problem again within a few days, you can bring it up.

Communication is also about listening. When the two of you are discussing an issue, make sure that you listen to what he's saying and that he is listening to you. Try to understand things from his perspective. Remember that when it comes to emotions, there's no such thing as right and wrong, whether they're his emotions or yours. This doesn't mean that you have to agree with everything he says to make him feel better. It just means that in a relationship, both people's feelings are important. Once you and your boyfriend both realize that, it makes compromise easier. And sometimes just talking about how you feel can help the other person understand you and cut down on conflict.

Communicating about problems can sometimes cause serious arguments. You and your boyfriend may be angry at each other sometimes. It's difficult to stay calm when

BOUNDARIES

One of the words you might hear people talk about when they discuss relationships is "boundaries." Boundaries are basically what they sound like. You draw lines around what you will allow in a relationship and what you won't. They can be physical (I will kiss, but not make out) or emotional (I will never let anyone call me a name, even as a joke). An example of a boundary is, "I will never tolerate him flirting with other girls." This doesn't mean that you'll automatically break up with him if he flirts with another girl (unless that's what you want to do). It does mean that you need to tell him that flirting with other girls is something you won't tolerate from him. Then, if he keeps doing it, you know he doesn't respect your feelings and it's time to break up.

Boundaries are important in any relationship because all people have different ideas of what relationships should be. They set up the "rules" for a relationship. Obviously, it's important to talk to you boyfriend about any boundaries that you have. You don't have to sit down at a table and hash them out at the beginning of the relationship, but it's important to discuss them as problems come up.

Remember that your boundaries are your own and are never right or wrong. You can even change them if you want. The important thing is that you learn what they are and how to set them. Part of growing up is learning to do this, and your first relationship is a great place to start.

you're upset about something important to you, but remember not to be insulting or hurtful. If he's insulting or hurtful during a conflict, be sure to tell him that he's hurting your feelings. If he continues to do the same things, you should consider breaking up.

Coming to an Agreement

Sometimes the best way to solve conflicts is to compromise. If you're arguing about what movie you should watch or where you should go eat, compromise is pretty simple. You can take turns going to different places, find a third option, or go see the movie you want to see with your friends and find something else to do with your boyfriend.

Emotional issues are a little trickier. This is another reason why honesty and communication are important. Sometimes you'll find that something is much more important to the other person than it is to you. In that case, it may be best for you to compromise, as long as doing so doesn't violate your personal values.

Remember that compromise is important, but don't just do it to avoid conflict. If you do that, you'll wind up resentful and unhappy. Don't compromise with the idea that he'll "owe" you, and make sure that you aren't the only one compromising for the sake of the relationship. The relationship exists to make both of you happy. Someone who truly cares about you won't ask you to change the most important, fundamental parts of yourself to make him happy.

Carrying Out Your Agreement

When you and your boyfriend do reach a compromise, make sure you carry out your portion of the agreement. If you feel resentful or upset about your compromise at any point in time, talk to your boyfriend about it. It's OK to change your mind if you realize that an agreement you've reached isn't working for you anymore, but it's important to communicate with him about it. If you don't, you're likely to have more conflicts in the future.

He should also stick to his word and not try to cause you to feel guilty, upset, or like you owe him for any compromises he's made.

When Should We Call It Quits?

Sometimes, no matter how hard one or both of you tries, you can't solve the problems in your relationship.

Here are some signs that it's time to break up:

- You're not happy when you're with him. Maybe you're constantly fighting, or not speaking, or maybe you're just not enjoying being around him. A relationship shouldn't make your life unhappy or difficult.
- He refuses to discuss problems. A relationship without communication isn't a relationship at all and can leave you confused and discouraged.
- He discusses problems but doesn't follow through on agreements that the two of you make. You need to be able to trust him to do what he says he will.
- One or both of you finds it difficult to compromise. Sometimes two people can be different enough that it's difficult for them to find common ground, no matter how much they like each other.
- He tries to push you into sexual activity, drugs, drinking, or anything else you may not be comfortable doing. Respect is an important part of any relationship, and anyone who pushes you into anything that violates your personal values probably doesn't respect you.

If you and your boyfriend are feeling distant from each other and not really talking any more, it's probably time to break up.

- He keeps crossing your boundaries, even after you've made them clear.
- He acts jealous and controlling. If he tries to control what you wear, who you talk to, or where you go, or accuses you of cheating or flirting with other boys when you haven't, it's definitely best to call it off. Controlling behavior can often get worse and can even lead to an abusive relationship.
- He is abusive. Sometimes it's difficult to tell if your relationship is abusive or not. If you think you (or a friend) might

be in an abusive relationship, check out the Web sites at the back of the book to learn more. Some signs of abusive behavior are:

- He insults or demeans you on purpose.
- He destroys your property.
- He threatens you, your loved ones, or your pets.
- He physically hurts you, your loved ones, or your pets.

If you think you are in an abusive relationship or feel threatened by your boyfriend in any way, talk to a trusted adult.

CHAPTER FOUR

BREAKING UP

No matter what age you are or how long you've dated some- one, breaking up is difficult. It's a good idea to talk to friends or even adults to help you get through it.

If You're Breaking Up with Him

As weird as it sounds, make sure you tell him you want to break up. Sometimes people don't do this. Instead, they basically start ignoring that person: they don't return calls, they avoid him in public, and they hope that the person takes the hint and just goes away. If you're tempted to break up with your soon-to-be-ex this way, think about how hurtful and confusing it would be if someone broke up with you like that. It may sound easier just to stop talking to him, but being honest and straightforward will make both of you feel better in the long run.

Breaking up face-to-face is difficult, but it's the best way to tell him it's over. You'll feel better if you tell him in person.

If you haven't talked to him yet, don't announce your breakup to anyone but close friends. Definitely don't announce it on Facebook or anywhere else where other people could see. You want to be sure that he hears about your breakup from you first. Hearing from someone else could be hurtful and embarrassing to him and could make the breakup more difficult. Plus, you could wind up looking mean in front of a large group of people for no good reason.

Break up face-to-face. It may be easier to text him or have a friend break up with him for you, but again, you'll feel better about yourself if you do it face-to-face. This also lets him know that you are serious about breaking up with him. If you're nervous, try practicing on your own or with a friend.

Don't be mean, but don't feel like you have to explain or justify yourself to him. A simple,

CAN I BREAK UP WITH HIM WITHOUT HURTING HIS FEELINGS?

Sometimes it can be really hard to break up with someone. Most people don't like hurting other people's feelings. Plus, girls often feel more pressure from society to be nice than boys do. You may feel tempted to drag the breakup process out or even stay in a relationship you're not happy in because you don't want to upset him.

The truth is that there is no way to break up with someone without causing at least a little temporary pain. Everyone is different and will react to breakups differently, but nobody likes being rejected. Make sure that you are honest and kind during your breakup—that's all you can do. His feelings are his own. How he reacts to a breakup is up to him.

Remember that you're doing what's best for you. You're also doing what's best for him because he deserves to be in relationship with a girl who truly wants to be his girlfriend. Think of it like pulling a baby tooth. It hurts less if you pull it out quickly, and something new will grow in its place.

"This isn't working for me anymore" is enough. If he's done something hurtful and you feel like you need to tell him how you feel, go ahead. It's up to you how much or how little you want to say.

If He's Breaking Up with You

You may feel angry, sad, surprised, betrayed, confused; no matter what, you're going to have some emotions

Rely on your friends to support you through a breakup. They're there to listen. When they have problems in their lives, you'll be there to listen, too.

that may be hard to deal with at first. Try as hard as you can to accept things gracefully and not say anything you'll regret later, but if you need to cry or yell, go ahead.

Breakups are especially difficult if he does it in a cruel way. Remind yourself that he's shown his true colors and you wouldn't want to be with a person who would treat someone else badly anyway. Keep how you feel now in mind when you break up with someone in the future and try to avoid what he did.

MY FRIEND WANTS TO DATE MY EX

Generally it's not good for friends to date friends' exes. It does happen sometimes, especially if you go to a small school or hang out in a group of guys and girls. Hopefully your friend talks to you before asking your ex out. If she doesn't, she's probably not a very good friend. If she does ask, it's up to you to decide how you feel about the situation. If the idea of them dating upsets you, then tell her. Obviously, you can't keep the two of them apart if they want to be together, but if she's a good friend, she'll have respect for your feelings. If your friend starts dating your ex and it stings a little, but they're respectful (it's been a long time since you've dated and neither one is a jerk to you), then it might be worth it to try to stay friends with her if you're really close to her. If it's too difficult for you emotionally, then you may have to end the friendship. It's never fun to lose a friend to a boy, but it happens sometimes. Just remember that you deserve to have friends who care about you and respect your feelings.

There isn't anything wrong with you if you've been rejected. It doesn't mean that you won't have another (and probably better) relationship in the future. Try to rely on friends and family members for support. The pain will pass eventually and you'll be a stronger person.

After You Break Up

It can be difficult seeing your ex at school or other places, especially if you know a lot of the same people. Remember that this will get easier, too, as time passes. Your ex may be hurting, too. Try not to act like a jerk, and if he acts like a jerk, don't take it personally. It's probably a good thing that you're not with him anymore.

It may be a while before you get over your breakup. In the meantime, do what you need to do to help yourself feel better. If you need to spend time alone, that's fine. If you need to cry, that's fine, too. If it helps you to hang out with your friends more, or throw yourself into schoolwork, or start an art project, that's fine, too. On the other hand, if you're ready to jump back into the pool and start dating again, that's OK, too. Only you can know how you feel and what you need.

And just keep in mind that, after a breakup, it will not make you feel any better to keep an eye on your ex via Facebook or Twitter. Even if you are the one who initiated the breakup, it's usually best to unfriend or unfollow him and keep your distance.

Eventually, you'll feel better. When you date again, try to think about what made you happy in your last relationship and what didn't. See if you can take some of those lessons and apply them to your new relationship.

And, of course, make sure it's a mutually enjoyable experience.

MYTHS AND FACTS

Myth: People who love each other never disagree.
Fact: Disagreements are a part of any relationship. You and your boyfriend have different personalities. You have different emotions. You were raised differently. No matter how alike you may be, you are still two separate, different people, and that's good! If the two of you were exactly alike and agreed on everything, your relationship would become boring. You'd never learn anything from each other. The important thing is that you work together to resolve your disagreements.

Myth: Guys are only interested in sex.
Fact: Everyone is different. Boys feel pressure to have sex, just as girls do. Many boys may just want to hang out and have fun. Make sure that both of you communicate about what you want. If your boyfriend is pressuring you to do something you don't want to, remember that there are boys out there who won't.

Myth: You're more mature if you have a boyfriend.
Fact: Having a boyfriend doesn't automatically make you more mature. Many mature women don't have boyfriends, and many immature women do. Being mature means that you know what you want and you're honest about it. In fact, it's more mature not to have a boyfriend if you don't want one. You can focus on things that you like. These things will help you to grow as a person.

10 GREAT QUESTIONS
TO ASK A GUIDANCE COUNSELOR

1. **WHAT SHOULD I DO IF MY PARENTS DISAPPROVE OF MY BOYFRIEND?**

2. **WHAT DO I DO IF MY FRIENDS DON'T LIKE MY BOYFRIEND?**

3. **WHAT SHOULD I DO IF OTHER PEOPLE ARE GOSSIPING ABOUT MY BOYFRIEND AND ME?**

4. **HOW SHOULD MY BOYFRIEND AND I ACT TOWARD EACH OTHER IN SCHOOL? FOR EXAMPLE, WILL WE GET INTO TROUBLE IF WE HOLD HANDS IN THE HALLWAY?**

5. **HOW SHOULD I DEAL WITH PRESSURE TO HAVE A SEXUAL RELATIONSHIP?**

6. **WHAT DO I DO IF MY BOYFRIEND IS MEAN TO ME OR MY FAMILY OR FRIENDS?**

7. **WHAT SHOULD I DO IF MY BOYFRIEND IS HAVING PROBLEMS IN SCHOOL, WITH HIS FAMILY, OR OTHER ISSUES?**

8. **WHAT HAPPENS IF MY FRIEND AND I ARE FIGHTING OVER THE SAME BOY?**

9. **HOW DO I KEEP MY RELATIONSHIP FROM DISTRACTING ME FROM SCHOOL?**

10. **HOW DO I ACT TOWARD MY EX WHEN I SEE HIM IN SCHOOL?**

GLOSSARY

boundaries Limits people set to keep themselves emotionally healthy.

communication The act of exchanging information.

compromise A deal in which one person gives up part of a demand to reach an agreement with another person.

conflict A disagreement or struggle that occurs when people have differences.

confront To meet face-to-face with someone, especially about a disagreement.

control To use influence to cause a person to do something or to keep a person from doing something that he or she might want to do.

emotion A strong feeling that usually has a physical response of some sort with it, like anger, which can cause people to be physically tense.

flirting Giving verbal and/or physical signs of interest in a romantic relationship with someone.

guilt-tripping A form of manipulation designed to make someone feel bad so that the person who is doing the guilt-tripping can get what he or she wants.

rejection When someone is turned down or excluded from a relationship.

relationship A connection between two people that may involve sharing thoughts, feelings, and experiences.

respect A positive feeling about someone, especially his or her abilities and personality.

sexting Sending sexually explicit texts or pictures via cell phone.

FOR MORE INFORMATION

Break the Cycle
5777 W. Century Boulevard, Suite 1150
Los Angeles, CA 90045
Web site: http://www.breakthecycle.org
Break the Cycle "engages, educates and empowers young people to
        build lives and communities free from domestic and dating vio-
        lence." Break the Cycle provides resources to determine if you are
        abused and trains young people in spotting and preventing abuse.

Dibble Institute
P.O. Box 7881
Berkeley, CA 94707-0881
Web site: http://www.dibbleinstitute.org
The Dibble Institute provides resources for teaching relationship skills
        to teens.

Girls for a Change
P.O. Box 1436
San Jose, CA 95109
Web site: http://www.girlsforachange.org
Girls for a Change mentors young women, teaching them self-
        confidence and the ability to speak out to create social change.

Girlshealth
8270 Willow Oaks Corporate Drive
Suite 301
Fairfax, VA 22031
Web site: http://www.girlshealth.gov
Girlshealth.gov provides resources and tips for young women about
        relationships and health.

Girls Inc.
120 Wall Street
New York, NY 10005-3902
Web site: http://www.girlsinc.org
Girls Inc. is a nonprofit organization with programs to help girls be
    strong and empowered. There are affiliates across the country.

Girl Talk
3490 Piedmont Road
Suite 1104
Atlanta, GA 30305
Web site: http://www.desiretoinspire.org
Girl Talk is an organization with chapters nationwide. Chapters hold
    weekly meetings in which high school girls mentor girls who are
    in middle school.

Healthy Teen Network
1501 Saint Paul Street, Suite 124
Baltimore, MD 21202
Web site: http://www.healthyteennetwork.org
Healthy Teen Network is an organization that focuses on teen health,
    especially preventing pregnancy.

Helping Our Teen Girls (HOTGirls)
3645 Marketplace Boulevard, #130-190
Atlanta, GA 30344
Web site: http://www.helpingourteengirls.org
This is a nonprofit organization devoted to educating underserved
    young women about health and media literacy using hip-hop and
    youth culture.

Smart-Girl
6825 E. Tennessee Avenue, Suite 637
Denver, CO 80224
Web site: http://www.smart-girl.org
Smart-Girl is an organization that seeks to help young women make
    healthy and empowering choices.

Youth Over Violence
1015 Wilshire Boulevard, Suite 200
Los Angeles, CA 90017
Web site: http://www.youthoverviolence.org
Youth Over Violence is an organization that works to eliminate domes-
    tic violence, sexual abuse, and rape by educating young people
    to change themselves and the world around them.

Web Sites

Due to the changing nature of Internet links, Rosen Publishing has devel-
oped an online list of Web sites related to the subject of this book. This
site is updated regularly. Please use this link to access the list:

http://www.rosenlinks.com/r101/bf

FOR FURTHER READING

Beck, Debra. *My Feet Aren't Ugly: A Girl's Guide to Loving Herself from the Inside Out.* New York, NY: Beaufort Books, 2007.

Brown, Lauren, ed. *Girls' Life Ultimate Guide to Surviving Middle School.* New York, NY: Scholastic Paperbacks, 2010.

Carrier, Julie Marie. *BeYOUtiful! The Ultimate Girl's and Young Woman's Guide to Discovering Your True Beauty, Gaining a Higher Self-Confidence and Developing Personal Success in All Areas of Your Life!* Las Vegas, NV: Positive Role Model Press, 2010.

Couwenhoven, Terri. *Growing Up: Choices and Changes in the Tween Years.* Bethesda, MD: Woodbine House, 2011.

Criswell, Patti Kelley. *A Smart Girl's Guide to Knowing What to Say.* Middleton, WI: American Girl, 2011.

Dunham, Deb. *Tween You and Me: A Preteen Guide to Becoming Your Best Self.* Maroochydore, Queensland, Australia: Empowered Publishing, 2009.

Farrell, Juliana, Beth Mayall, and Megan Howard. *Middle School: The Real Deal: From Cafeteria Food to Combination Locks.* New York, NY: HarperCollins, 2007.

Flynn, Sarah Wassner, ed. *Girls' Life Guide to a Drama-Free Life.* New York, NY: Scholastic Paperbacks, 2010.

Flynn, Sarah Wassner, ed. *Girls' Life Guide to Being the Most Amazing You.* New York, NY: Scholastic Paperbacks, 2010.

Fox, Annie. *Be Confident in Who You Are.* Minneapolis, MN: Free Spirit Publishing, 2008.

Kilpatrick, Haley, and Whitney Joiner. *The Drama Years: Real Girls Talk About Surviving Middle School—Bullies, Brands, Body Image, and More.* New York, NY: Free Press, 2012.

Macavinta, Courtney, and Andrea Vander Pluym. *Respect: A Girl's Guide to Getting Respect and Dealing When Your Line Is Crossed.* Minneapolis, MN: Free Spirit Publishing, 2005.

Moss, Wendy L. *Being Me: A Kid's Guide to Boosting Confidence and Self-Esteem.* Washington, DC: Magination Press, 2010.

Mostache, Harriet S., and Karen Unger. *Too Old for This, Too Young for That! Your Survival Guide for the Middle School Years.* Minnesota, MN: Free Spirit Publishing, 2010.

Mysko, Claire. *Girls Inc. Presents: You're Amazing! A No-Pressure Guide to Being Your Best Self.* Avon, MA: Adams Media, 2008.

Smith, Keri, and Sarah O'Leary Burmingham. *Boyology: A Teen Girl's Crash Course in All Things Boy.* San Francisco, CA: Chronicle Books, 2009.

Winters, Ben H. *The Worst-Case Scenario Handbook: Surviving Middle School.* San Francisco, CA: Chronicle Books, 2009.

BIBLIOGRAPHY

American Academy of Pediatrics. "Talking to Kids About Social Media and Sexting." March 2, 2011. Retrieved October 2, 2011 (http://www.aap.org/advocacy/releases/june09socialmedia.htm).

Carter, Carol. *People Smarts for Teens: Becoming Emotionally Intelligent.* Denver, CO: Lifebound, 2006.

Cooperative Extension Education in Agriculture and Home Economics, University of Delaware. "Talking with Your Preteen About Sexuality." Retrieved September 25, 2011 (http://ag.udel.edu/extension/fam/FM/issue/preteensexuality.htm).

Domestic Violence Resource Centre Victoria. "Love or Control?" Retrieved September 3, 2011 (http://lovegoodbadugly.com/category/love-control).

Fogarty, Kate. "Teens and Dating: Tips for Parents and Professionals." October 2006. Retrieved August 2, 2011 (http://edis.ifas.ufl.edu/fy851).

Fox, Annie. *The Teen Survival Guide to Dating & Relating: Real-World Advice for Teens on Guys, Girls, Growing Up, and Getting Along.* Minneapolis, MN: Free Spirit Publishing, 2005.

Hartley-Brewer, Elizabeth. *Praising Girls Well: 100 Tips for Parents and Teachers.* Cambridge, MA: Da Capo Press, 2006.

Hartley-Brewer, Elizabeth. *Talking to Tweens: Getting It Right Before It Gets Rocky with Your 8- to 12-Year-Old.* Cambridge, MA: Da Capo Press, 2005.

Levy, Barrie. *Love in Danger.* 3rd ed. New York, NY: Seal Press, 2006.

Mayo Clinic Staff. "Sex Education: Talking to Your School-Aged Children About Sex." April 30, 2011. Retrieved September 14, 2011 (http://www.mayoclinic.com/health/sex-education/CC00076).

Mulford, Carrie, and Peggy C. Giordano. "Teen Dating Violence: A Closer Look at Adolescent Romantic Relationships." October 27,

2008. Retrieved August 7, 2011 (http://www.nij.gov/journals/261/teen-dating-violence.htm).

National Center for Injury Prevention and Control, Division of Violence Prevention. "Talking to Teens About Healthy Relationships." February 22, 2011. Retrieved August 7, 2011 (http://www.cdc.gov/features/chooserespect/).

Olsen, Deborah Pike. "Having the Sex Talk: Is Your Tween Too Sexy Too Soon?" Retrieved September 14, 2011 (http://www.parenting.com/article/sex-talk-tweens).

Pelzer, Dave. *Help Yourself for Teens: Real-Life Advice for Real-Life Challenges.* New York, NY: Penguin Group, 2005.

Perlstein, Linda. "A User's Guide to Middle School Romance." *Washington Post Magazine*, February 13, 2005, p. W20.

Rankin, Lissa. "How to Talk to Your Tween—and Be Heard." April 19, 2011. Retrieved October 2, 2011 (http://www.care2.com/greenliving/how-to-talk-to-your-tween-girl-and-be-heard.html).

Ross, Julie A. *How to Hug a Porcupine: Negotiating the Prickly Points of the Tween Years.* Columbus, OH: McGraw-Hill, 2008.

Stabiner, Karen. *Reclaiming Our Daughters: What Parenting a Pre-Teen Taught Me About Real Girls.* New York, NY: Seal Press, 2007.

Steinberg, Lawrence. "Talking to Your Teen About Sex." February 14, 2011. Retrieved September 25, 2011 (http://www.psychologytoday.com/blog/you-and-your-adolescent/201102/talking-your-teen-about-sex).

Walsh, David. *Why Do They Act That Way? A Survival Guide to the Adolescent Brain for You and Your Teen.* New York, NY: Free Press, 2005.

INDEX

About the Author

Katie Hentges is an author of books for teens. She lives in Portland, Oregon.

Photo Credits

Cover, p. 1 Dmitriy Shironosov/Shutterstock; pp. 3 (top), 10 Jack Hollingsworth/Photodisc/Thinkstock; pp. 3 (bottom), 29 Stockbyte/Thinkstock; pp. 4–5, 6, 15, 23, 30 istockphoto.com/Thinkstock; p. 7 Jupiterimages/Photos.com/Thinkstock; p. 8 Photodisc/Thinkstock; p. 13 Nivek Neslo/Taxi/Getty Images; pp.16, 22, 24 Comstock/Thinkstock; p. 17 Gary Houlder/Taxi/Getty Images; p. 19 Steve Mason/Photodisc/Thinkstock; p. 21 Hemera/Thinkstock; p. 31 SW Productions/Photodisc/Getty Images; p. 33 Image Source/Getty Images; © istockphoto.com/kemie (interior graphics); © istockphoto.com/stereohype (back cover background, interior graphics).

Designer: Michael Moy; Editor: Bethany Bryan;
Photo Researcher: Marty Levick